GERMANY NATIONAL GEOGRAPHIC ROAD ATLAS MAP 2025

DISCOVER GERMANY'S SCENIC ROUTES, HISTORIC LANDMARKS AND HIDDEN GEMS WITH DETAILED MAPS, DRIVING TIPS AND MUST SEE DESTINATIONS

KARL STIELER

Contents

Munich

Cologne

Berlin

Introduction

Travel Companion for Navigating Germany Roads and Cities

Germany is a country that seamlessly blends history, culture, and modern innovation with some of the most efficient infrastructure in the world. Whether you're cruising down the Autobahn, exploring medieval towns, or navigating through the dynamic streets of Berlin, having a reliable road map and travel guide is essential for making the most of your journey.

This Germany National Geographic Atlas Road Map 2025 is designed to be your ultimate travel companion whether you're a first-time visitor, a seasoned road-tripper, or a local exploring new destination. It goes beyond just providing maps; it offers in-depth regional insights, driving tips, and up-to-date travel regulations to ensure your journey through Germany is smooth, efficient, and enriching.

With this book in hand, you will

Navigate Germany with confidence: detailed maps, route suggestions, and road conditions for 2025.

Discover hidden gems: beyond tourist hotspots, explore charming villages, scenic byways, and cultural treasures.

Plan your journey wisely: learn about fuel stops, charging stations, rest areas, and road trip-friendly accommodations.

Stay informed: up-to-date regulations, toll-free routes, emissions zones, and essential safety tips.

Germany's rich landscapes, from the Bavarian Alps to the coastal beauty of the Baltic Sea, are best experienced by road. This book ensures that every mile you drive is a memorable and well-prepared adventure.

How to Use This Atlas

Understanding Maps, Symbols, and Navigation Tips

This guide is more than just a collection of maps—it's a comprehensive tool to help you efficiently interpret and use Germany's road network. Whether you're traveling by car, campervan, or motorcycle, understanding the symbols, signs, and navigation tips will make your journey stress-free and enjoyable.

Map Features & Symbols

Road Types & Colors: Major highways (Autobahns) are marked in blue, national roads in yellow and scenic routes in green.

Toll Roads & Free Routes: Most highways in Germany are toll-free for cars, but trucks have designated toll routes. This guide highlights key toll roads and alternative free routes.

Emissions Zones: Cities with environmental restrictions (such as Berlin and Munich) have low-emission zones, requiring a special permit to enter. Maps will indicate where these zones are.

Rest Areas & Fuel Station: Locations of Autobahn service stations, charging points for electric vehicles, and major rest stops.

Scenic Viewpoints & Attractions: Marked spots where you can stop to take in breathtaking landscapes or visit cultural landmarks.

Navigation Tips

Using GPS & Digital Maps: While Google Maps, Waze, and Apple Maps are widely used, having a physical map or offline GPS option is recommended for areas with weak internet signals.

Understanding German Road Signs: While most signs follow universal European symbols, knowing key German terms like "Ausfahrt" (Exit) and "Umleitung" (Detour) will be useful.

Speed Limit Awareness: Germany's Autobahn has unrestricted speed sections, but many areas now have regulated limits. This guide will clarify speed limits for different roads.

Parking & Urban Navigation: Some cities have Park & Ride options to reduce traffic congestion. Maps will highlight parking zones, paid parking areas, and pedestrian-only streets.

By familiarizing yourself with these symbols and tips, you can plan smarter routes, avoid roadblocks, and make the most of your time on the road.

Updated Roads, Scenic Routes, and Travel Regulations

Every years Germany makes adjustments to its road infrastructure, environmental policies, and travel regulations. This section highlights key updates for 2025 that travelers should know before setting out on their journey.

1. Autobahn & Roadway Expansions

Several highway expansions and bridge reconstructions were completed in 2025 to reduce congestion on major routes, particularly around Berlin, Frankfurt, and Hamburg.

Smart highways now integrate digital traffic monitoring, automatically adjusting speed limits in high-traffic areas.

2. Environmental & Low-Emission Zones

New emissions restrictions have been introduced in cities like Stuttgart and Düsseldorf, requiring vehicles to have a valid Umweltplakette (environmental badge) to enter certain districts.

Expansion of green energy charging stations along the Autobahn, making long-distance EV travel easier.

3. New Scenic & Themed Routes

Introduction of the "Historic Wine Route", connecting Germany's most famous vineyards with new rest stops and cultural experiences.

Expansion of cycling friendly roadways, particularly in Bavaria and the Black Forest, allowing for scenic cycling alongside road trips.

4. Travel & Road Safety Updates

New speed regulations for specific sections of the Autobahn, particularly in high-traffic areas, to improve safety.

Updates to roadside emergency services, including multilingual support for international travelers.

Staying updated on these changes ensures that you travel legally, efficiently, and with peace of mind.

Essential Travel Information

Time Zones, Currency, Emergency Contacts, and Useful Apps

Before hitting the road, having essential travel information at your fingertips will help you avoid unnecessary stress and make your journey smoother.

1. Time Zones

Germany operates on Central European Time (CET):

Standard Time: UTC +1

Daylight Savings Time (March - October): UTC +2

Always check time zone differences if crossing borders into France, Switzerland, Austria, or Poland.

2. Currency & Payments

The official currency is the Euro (€).

Credit and debit cards are widely accepted, but some smaller towns and rural areas still prefer cash payments.

Contactless & Mobile Payments: Apple Pay, Google Pay, and local German apps like Payback Pay are commonly used.

3. Emergency Contacts

General Emergency Number: 112 (for police, fire, and ambulance services).

Roadside Assistance

ADAC (Germany's largest auto club) - Dial +49 89 222 222

Freeway emergency phones: Located every 2 kilometers on the Autobahn.

Tourist Helplines:

Germany's official tourism board - +49 30 250 02333

Local police for lost passports - 110

4. Useful Apps for Road Trips

Navigation & Traffic Updates

Google Maps: An indispensable tool for navigation, Google Maps not only provides detailed directions but also offers real-time traffic updates, route options, and points of interest along your way.

Roadtrippers: Designed specifically for road travel, Roadtrippers lets you create detailed itineraries and discover attractions, restaurants, and hidden gems along your route.

Waze: This community-driven navigation app offers real-time updates from other drivers on traffic conditions, hazards, and police presence.

Fuel & Charging Stations:

Tank & Rast: Locates Autobahn fuel stations and rest stops.

Plug Share: Lists EV charging points.

Language & Translation

Google Translate: Helpful for road signs and conversations.

DeepL: This provides more accurate translations for longer texts.

Language Assistance: Encountering a language barrier while traveling can be daunting. Our app includes essential phrases and translations for quick communication, making your interactions smoother and more enjoyable.

Detailed Road Maps: Navigate through Germany's cities, rural areas, and hidden gems with precise and easy-to-read maps, ensuring you never lose your way.

Having these essential tools on hand will make navigating Germany stress-free and enjoyable.

This introduction sets the foundation for the rest of the book; ensuring travelers have all the essential information before hitting the road.

Germany

SCAN HERE

HOW TO USE QR CODE

- Open your phone's camera app or download scanner app from play store or apple store
- Point the camera at the QR code for a few seconds (no need to take a photo).
- A link should appear on the display, leading you to the location of the code

Chapter 1

Germany at a Glance

Germany is a country of contrast where medieval castles coexist with cutting-edge technology, where vast forests give way to bustling cities, and where centuries-old traditions thrive alongside a modern, cosmopolitan society. Whether you're exploring the snow capped Alps, the vineyard-covered valleys of the Rhine, or the vibrant urban life of Berlin, understanding Germany's geography, climate, cultural identity, and transportation systems will help you travel smarter and experience the country more deeply.

Overview of Germany's Regions, Landscapes and Seasonal Weather Patterns

Germany's Geographic Diversity

Germany is centrally located in Europe, sharing borders with nine countries: Denmark to the north, Poland and the Czech Republic to the east, Austria and Switzerland to the south, and France, Luxembourg, Belgium, and the Netherlands to the west. This strategic position has shaped Germany into a cultural and economic powerhouse, acting as a bridge between Western and Eastern Europe.

Germany covers approximately 357,000 square kilometers (138,000 square miles) and boasts an incredibly diverse landscape, ranging from coastal plains in the north to rugged alpine peaks in the south. The country is divided into 16 federal states (Bundesländer), each with its own distinct geography and cultural identity.

Key Geographical Regions

Northern Germany (Coastal Lowlands & the North Sea/Baltic Coast)

Characterized by flat plains, sandy beaches, and coastal islands.

Major cities: Hamburg, Bremen, Kiel, Rostock.

Home to the Wadden Sea, a UNESCO World Heritage Site with unique tidal ecosystems.

Strong maritime culture with bustling port cities and fresh seafood cuisine.

Central Germany (Rolling Hills & River Valleys)

Features vineyards, dense forests, and picturesque river landscapes.

Major cities: Frankfurt, Cologne, Leipzig, Dresden.

The Rhine, Main, and Elbe Rivers flow through this region, creating stunning scenic routes.

Home to the Black Forest (Schwarzwald) and Germany wine growing regions.

Southern Germany (The Alps & Bavaria's Lakes)

Marked by mountainous terrain, alpine lakes, and charming villages.

Major cities: Munich, Stuttgart, Nuremberg.

The Bavarian Alps provide some of the best hiking and skiing in Europe.

Fairy-tale castles like Neuschwanstein are scattered across the region.

Eastern Germany (Historic Towns & Lowlands)

Defined by historic cities, cultural heritage, and nature reserves.

Major cities: Berlin, Dresden, Weimar, Leipzig.

The region has a rich history, from the former Prussian Empire to the Cold War division.

Features vast forests and natural parks, such as Saxon Switzerland.

Germany's Climate & Seasonal Weather Patterns

Germany experiences a temperate seasonal climate, meaning weather conditions change significantly throughout the year.

Spring (March-May)

Temperatures: 10-20°C (50-68°F).

Nature comes alive with blooming cherry blossoms and vineyards turning green.

A great time for outdoor sightseeing before the peak summer crowds arrive.

Summer (June - August)

Temperatures: 20-35°C (68-95°F), with occasional heatwaves.

Ideal for beach trips to the Baltic Sea, hiking in the Alps, and beer gardens in Bavaria.

Major cities like Berlin, Munich, and Hamburg host vibrant festivals.

Autumn (September - November)

Temperatures: 10-20°C (50-68°F).

The Rhine Valley and Black Forest are covered in golden foliage, making for spectacular road trips.

The season of Oktoberfest in Munich and wine festivals in the Moselle region.

Winter (December - February)

Temperatures: -5 to 5°C (23-41°F), colder in the Alps.

The Alps offer world class skiing while German cities host magical Christmas markets.

Snow-covered castles and villages provide storybook winter scenery.

Understanding Germany's geography and climate will help you pack appropriately, plan your itinerary according to the seasons, and make the most of your travel experience.

Traditional Festivals & Events

Germany is renowned for its festive culture, with a mix of historic, religious, and regional celebrations throughout the year.

1. Oktoberfest: One of the most famous festivals globally, Oktoberfest takes place in Munich from late September to the first weekend in October. This 16 to 18 day folk festival attracts millions of visitors who come to enjoy traditional Bavarian beer, hearty cuisine, and lively music.

2. Carnival (Karneval/Fasching): Carnival season, particularly popular in Cologne, Düsseldorf, and Mainz, culminates in a series of parades and celebrations before Lent. The festivities begin on November 11 and reach their peak in February or March.

3. Christmas Markets (Weihnachtsmärkte): During the Advent season, towns and cities across Germany come alive with festive Christmas markets. These markets typically open around late November and continue until Christmas Eve.

4. Berlin International Film Festival (Berlinale): Held annually in February the Berlinale is one of the world's leading film festivals. It showcases a diverse range of films from around the globe, featuring both established filmmakers and new talent.

5. Landesgartenschau (State Garden Show): These regional horticultural exhibitions are held every two years in different states throughout Germany, showcasing stunning garden designs, landscape architecture, and floral displays.

Historical & Cultural Influences

Medieval heritage: Castles, half-timbered towns, and cobblestone streets are reminders of Germany's medieval past.

Music & literature: Germany was home to Beethoven, Bach, Goethe, and the Brothers Grimm.

Post-war transformation: Once divided, Germany rebuilt itself into a global leader in technology, sustainability, and innovation.

Transportation Overview: Highways (Autobahn), Regional Roads, Public Transport, and Rental Car Options

1. The Autobahn: Germany's Legendary Highway System

Famous for sections with no speed limits, but many areas have speed restrictions (typically 130 km/h or lower).

Well-maintained, toll-free for cars, and includes rest areas with fuel, food, and lodging.

Traffic laws require driving in the right lane unless overtaking.

2. Regional Roads & Scenic Drives

Romantic Road: A picturesque drive through Bavaria, passing castles and medieval towns.

Wine Route Weinstraße: A drive through Germany premier vineyard regions.

Alpine Road: A breathtaking mountain drive in southern Bavaria.

3. Public Transportation

An efficient train system (Deutsche Bahn) connects cities with high-speed ICE trains.

Regional buses & trams provide affordable options in smaller towns.

Underground (U-Bahn) & suburban (S-Bahn) trains are available in major cities.

4. Rental Car & Driving Tips

Rental cars are available at airports and major cities. A valid driver's license and passport are required.

Many cities have low-emission zones, meaning certain vehicles need an environmental sticker.

Fuel stations are self-service, and prices fluctuate. Diesel is often cheaper than gasoline.

With this foundation of geography, culture, and transportation, you're ready to explore Germany efficiently and enjoyably.

Hamburg

SCAN HERE

HOW TO USE QR CODE

- Open your phone's camera app or download scanner app from play store or apple store
- Point the camera at the QR code for a few seconds (no need to take a photo).
- A link should appear on the display, leading you to the location of the code

Bremen

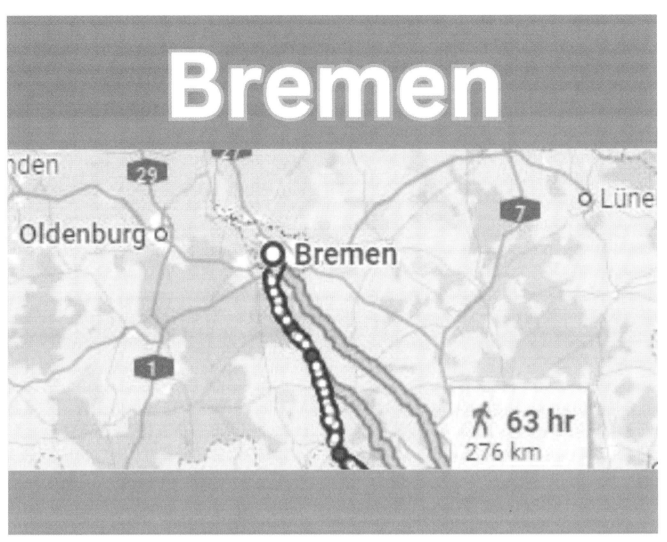

SCAN HERE

HOW TO USE QR CODE

- Open your phone's camera app or download scanner app from play store or apple store
- Point the camera at the QR code for a few seconds (no need to take a photo).
- A link should appear on the display, leading you to the location of the code

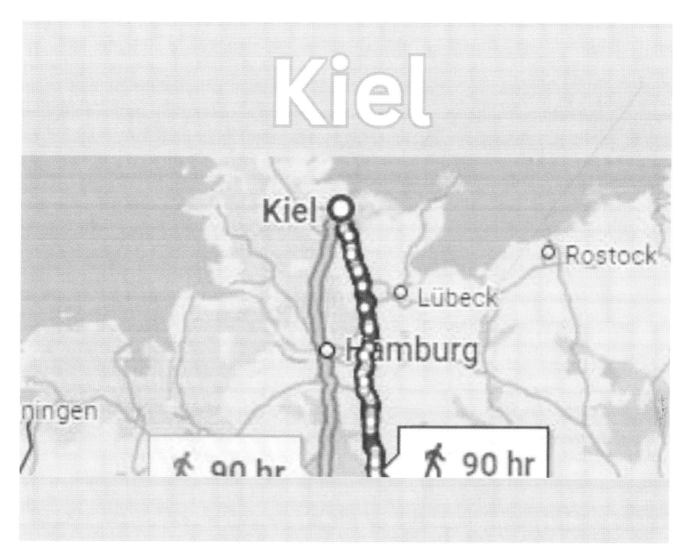

SCAN HERE

HOW TO USE QR CODE

- Open your phone's camera app or download scanner app from play store or apple store
- Point the camera at the QR code for a few seconds (no need to take a photo).
- A link should appear on the display, leading you to the location of the code

Rostock

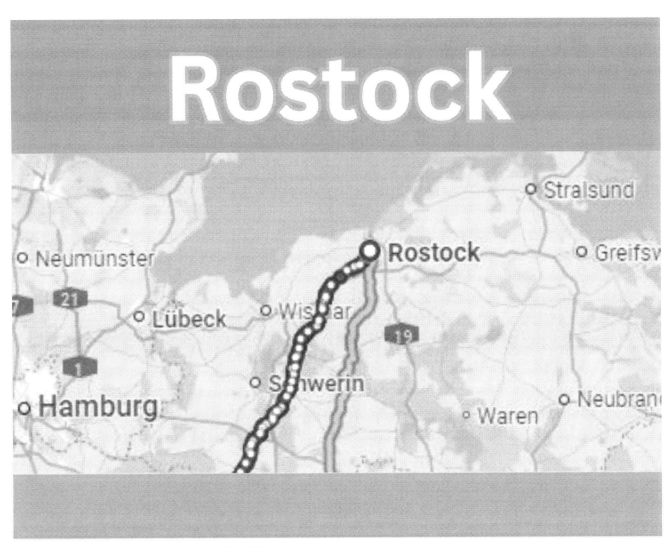

SCAN HERE

HOW TO USE QR CODE

- Open your phone's camera app or download scanner app from play store or apple store
- Point the camera at the QR code for a few seconds (no need to take a photo).
- A link should appear on the display, leading you to the location of the code

Frankfurt

SCAN HERE

HOW TO USE QR CODE

- Open your phone's camera app or download scanner app from play store or apple store
- Point the camera at the QR code for a few seconds (no need to take a photo).
- A link should appear on the display, leading you to the location of the code

Cologne

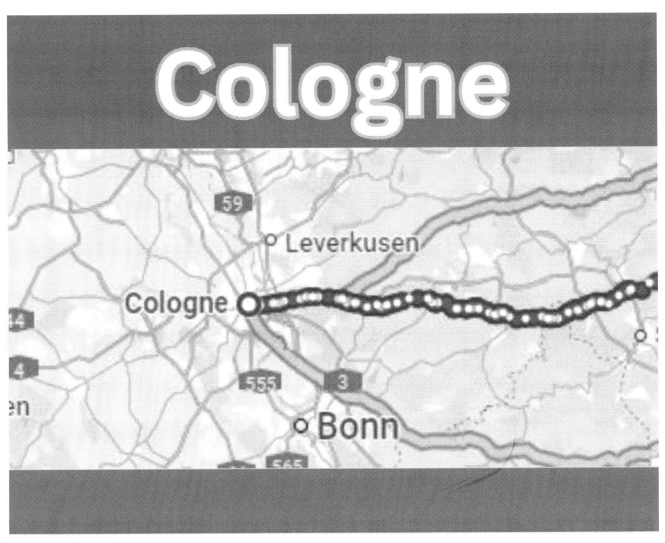

SCAN HERE

HOW TO USE QR CODE

- Open your phone's camera app or download scanner app from play store or apple store
- Point the camera at the QR code for a few seconds (no need to take a photo).
- A link should appear on the display, leading you to the location of the code

Leipzig

SCAN HERE

HOW TO USE QR CODE

- Open your phone's camera app or download scanner app from play store or apple store
- Point the camera at the QR code for a few seconds (no need to take a photo).
- A link should appear on the display, leading you to the location of the code

Dresden

SCAN HERE

HOW TO USE QR CODE

- Open your phone's camera app or download scanner app from play store or apple store
- Point the camera at the QR code for a few seconds (no need to take a photo).
- A link should appear on the display, leading you to the location of the code

Munich

SCAN HERE

HOW TO USE QR CODE

- Open your phone's camera app or download scanner app from play store or apple store
- Point the camera at the QR code for a few seconds (no need to take a photo).
- A link should appear on the display, leading you to the location of the code

Stuttgart

SCAN HERE

HOW TO USE QR CODE

- Open your phone's camera app or download scanner app from play store or apple store
- Point the camera at the QR code for a few seconds (no need to take a photo).
- A link should appear on the display, leading you to the location of the code

Nuremberg

SCAN HERE

HOW TO USE QR CODE

- Open your phone's camera app or download scanner app from play store or apple store
- Point the camera at the QR code for a few seconds (no need to take a photo).
- A link should appear on the display, leading you to the location of the code

Berlin

SCAN HERE

HOW TO USE QR CODE

- Open your phone's camera app or download scanner app from play store or apple store
- Point the camera at the QR code for a few seconds (no need to take a photo).
- A link should appear on the display, leading you to the location of the code

Weimar

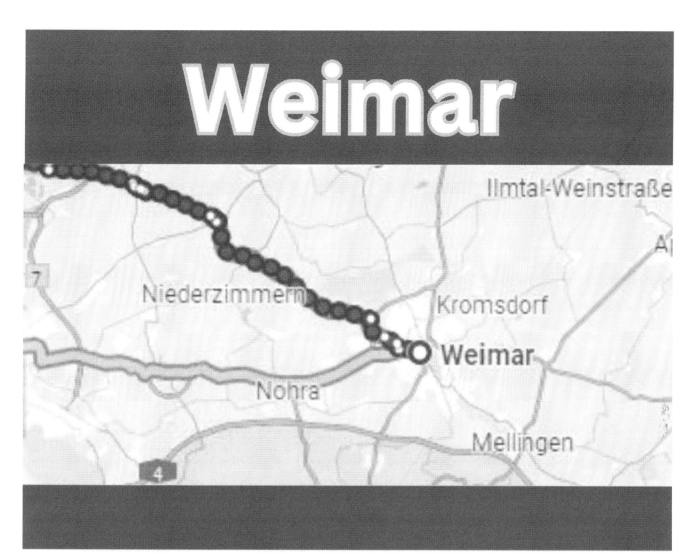

SCAN HERE

HOW TO USE QR CODE

- Open your phone's camera app or download scanner app from play store or apple store
- Point the camera at the QR code for a few seconds (no need to take a photo).
- A link should appear on the display, leading you to the location of the code

Chapter 2

Regional Highlights Landmarks, Nature, & History

Germany's diverse regions each offer unique cultural, historical, and natural treasures. From the port city charm of Hamburg to the fairy-tale castles of Bavaria, and from Berlin's iconic landmarks to the vineyard-covered Rhine Valley, each region tells a different story of Germany's past and present. Here are must-visit cities, stunning landscapes, and historical sites that define Germany's rich heritage and scenic beauty.

Northern Germany

Northern Germany is defined by its maritime culture, coastal landscapes, and historic hanseatic cities. With charming old towns, vast heath lands, and two unique coastlines (the North Sea and the Baltic Sea), this region is perfect for those who love both history and nature.

1. Hamburg: The Gateway to the World

Germany's second-largest city and biggest port, Hamburg is a dynamic blend of industrial power and cultural richness.

Speicherstad: A UNESCO-listed warehouse district with red-brick buildings and canals.

Elbe philharmonic hall: A striking modern concert hall with panoramic city views.

Reeperbahn: The famous nightlife district, once a haunt for The Beatles.

Harbor Boat Tour: Explore Hamburg maritime heart by cruising its massive port.

Bremen & Lower Saxony

Bremen: A medieval gem known for the Bremen Town Musicians statue, Schnoor Quarter, and historic Rathaus (Town Hall).

Lüneburg Heath: A stunning purple heather-covered landscape, best visited in late summer.

Harz Mountains: A region of half-timbered villages, scenic hiking trails, and the legendary Brocken peak.

Schleswig-Holstein: The North Sea & Baltic Coasts

Lübeck: A UNESCO-listed hanseatic town with medieval architecture.

Sylt: A North Sea island with pristine beaches and upscale resorts.

Wadden Sea: A unique tidal ecosystem and UNESCO World Heritage Site.

Eastern Germany

The historical heart of Germany, Eastern Germany, is where you'll find Berlin's powerful history, Saxony's Baroque beauty, and Thuringia's literary legacy.

1. Berlin: Where History Meets Modernity

Brandenburg Gate: Germany's most famous landmark, symbolizing unity.

The Berlin Wall & East Side Gallery: A preserved section of the Cold War-era wall, now a vibrant open-air art gallery.

Museum Island: Home to the Pergamon Museum, the Neues Museum, and other world-class institutions.

2. Saxony & Dresden

Dresden: The "Florence on the Elbe," famous for its Baroque architecture, including the Zwinger Palace and Frauenkirche.

Saxon Switzerland National Park: A breathtaking region of sandstone cliffs, deep valleys, and scenic hiking routes.

3. Thuringia: Castles & Cultural Heritage

Wartburg Castle: A UNESCO site where Martin Luther translated the Bible.

Weimar: The birthplace of Goethe, Schiller, and the Bauhaus movement.

Erfurt: A charming medieval town with beautiful half-timbered houses and the impressive Erfurt Cathedral.

Western Germany

Western Germany is a region rich in history, culture, and economic prowess, shaping the identity of the nation as a whole. This area, known for its vibrant cities and picturesque landscapes, stretches from the borders of France and Belgium to the west, extending to the industrious Rhine Valley an area renowned for its industrial heritage.

1. Cologne & the Rhineland

Cologne Cathedral: A Gothic masterpiece and UNESCO World Heritage Site.

Rhine Valley: A region of vineyards, historic castles and picturesque river cruises.

Drachenfels Castle: A legendary castle with panoramic views of the Rhine.

2. Frankfurt

Römerberg: A historic square with medieval half-timbered houses.

Goethe House: The birthplace of Germany greatest writer, Johann Wolfgang von Goethe.

Main Tower: This offers stunning panoramic views of Frankfurt's skyline.

3. Trier & Saarland

Trier: Germany's oldest city, with well-preserved Roman ruins like Porta Nigra.

Saarland: Influenced by French culture, known for fine cuisine and the scenic Saar River Loop.

Moselle Valley: A wine lover's paradise, with charming villages and steep vineyard slopes.

Southern Germany is a region of alpine beauty, fairy-tale castles, and rich traditions

1. Bavaria: Castles, Beer Gardens, & Alpine Wonders

Munich: The capital of Bavaria, famous for Oktoberfest, Marienplatz, and the English Garden.

Neuschwanstein Castle: The real life inspiration for Disney's Cinderella Castle.

The Bavarian Alps: Perfect for hiking, skiing and breathtaking mountain views.

2. Stuttgart & the Black Forest

Mercedes-Benz & Porsche Museum: Celebrating Germany's automotive excellence.

The Black Forest: A region of dense forests, cuckoo clocks, and spa towns like Baden-Baden.

Scenic Drives: The Black Forest High Road offers stunning views of valleys and traditional villages.

3. Lake Constance: A Waterside Paradise

Borders Austria & Switzerland, offering panoramic alpine views.

Lindau: A charming town with colorful waterfront buildings.

Reichenau Island: is A UNESCO listed Island known for medieval monasteries and vineyards.

Perfect for cycling, sailing, and summer getaways.

Germany's regional diversity ensures that every traveler can find something unique to explore, from urban adventures to nature retreats. Whether you're drawn to Hamburg's portside charm, Berlin's history, the castles of Bavaria, or the vineyards of the Rhine Valley, this guide provides a starting point for an unforgettable journey.

Hamburg

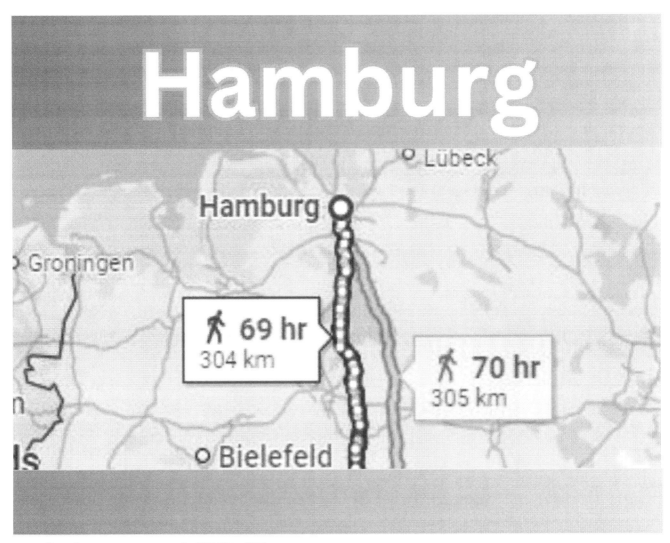

SCAN HERE

HOW TO USE QR CODE

- Open your phone's camera app or download scanner app from play store or apple store
- Point the camera at the QR code for a few seconds (no need to take a photo).
- A link should appear on the display, leading you to the location of the code

Speicherstadt

Speicherstadt

Reeperbahn

Bremen

SCAN HERE

HOW TO USE QR CODE

- Open your phone's camera app or download scanner app from play store or apple store
- Point the camera at the QR code for a few seconds (no need to take a photo).
- A link should appear on the display, leading you to the location of the code

Lüneburg Heath

Harz Mountains

Lübeck

SCAN HERE

HOW TO USE QR CODE

- Open your phone's camera app or download scanner app from play store or apple store
- Point the camera at the QR code for a few seconds (no need to take a photo).
- A link should appear on the display, leading you to the location of the code

Sylt

Berlin

SCAN HERE

HOW TO USE QR CODE

- Open your phone's camera app or download scanner app from play store or apple store
- Point the camera at the QR code for a few seconds (no need to take a photo).
- A link should appear on the display, leading you to the location of the code

Brandenburg Gate

Museum Island

Saxony

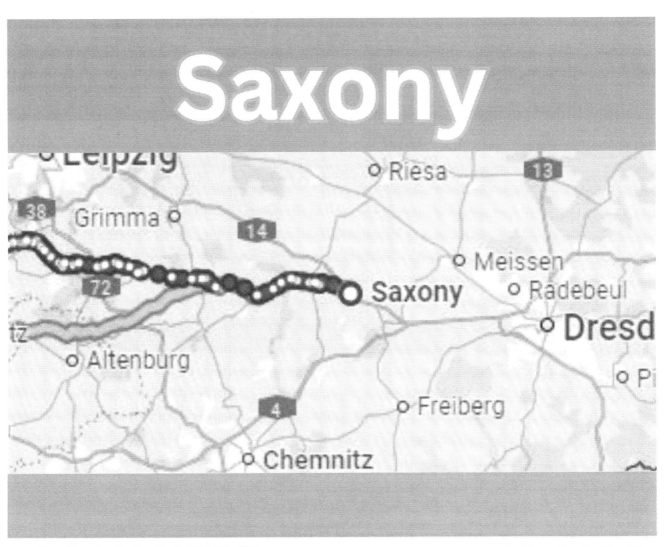

SCAN HERE

HOW TO USE QR CODE

- Open your phone's camera app or download scanner app from play store or apple store
- Point the camera at the QR code for a few seconds (no need to take a photo).
- A link should appear on the display, leading you to the location of the code

Dresden

SCAN HERE

HOW TO USE QR CODE

- Open your phone's camera app or download scanner app from play store or apple store
- Point the camera at the QR code for a few seconds (no need to take a photo).
- A link should appear on the display, leading you to the location of the code

Zwinger Palace

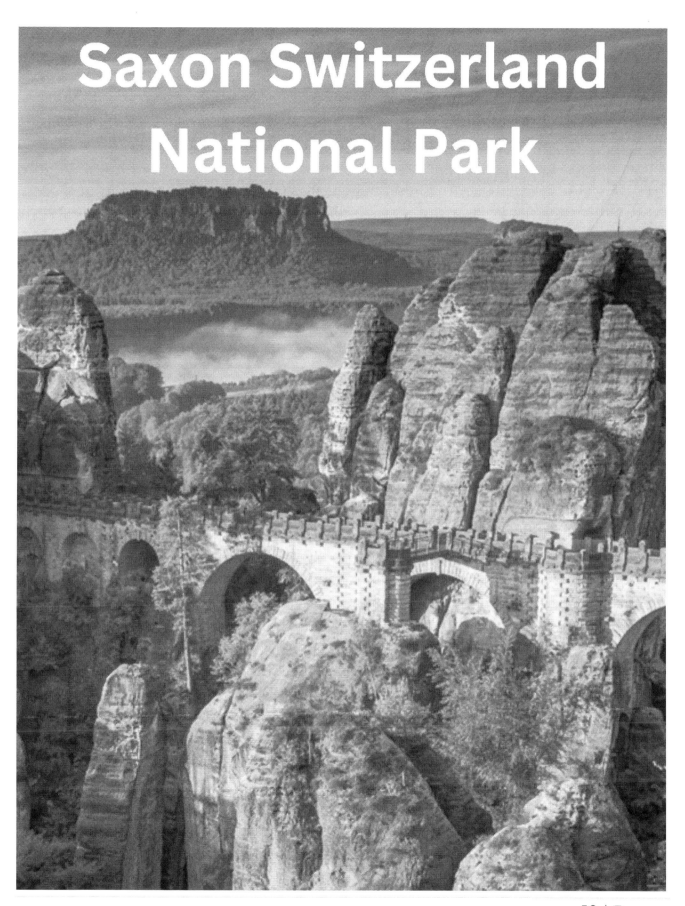

Saxon Switzerland National Park

Wartburg Castle

Erfurt

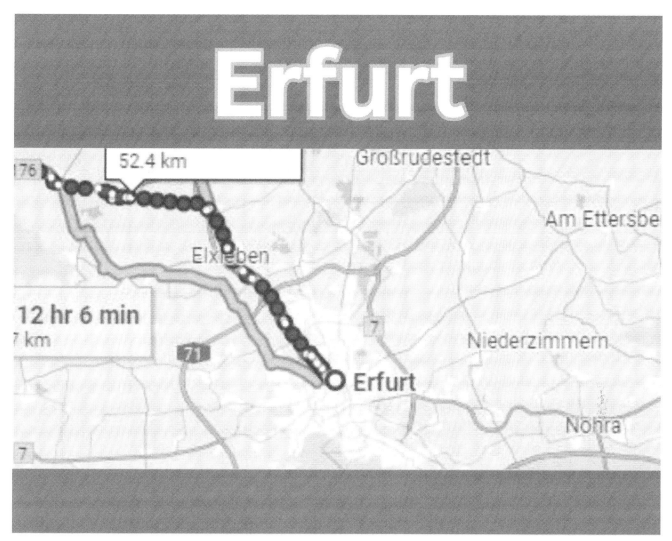

SCAN HERE

HOW TO USE QR CODE

- Open your phone's camera app or download scanner app from play store or apple store
- Point the camera at the QR code for a few seconds (no need to take a photo).
- A link should appear on the display, leading you to the location of the code

Rhine Valley

Drachenfels Castle

Frankfurt

SCAN HERE

HOW TO USE QR CODE

- Open your phone's camera app or download scanner app from play store or apple store
- Point the camera at the QR code for a few seconds (no need to take a photo).
- A link should appear on the display, leading you to the location of the code

Römerberg

Goethe House

Trier

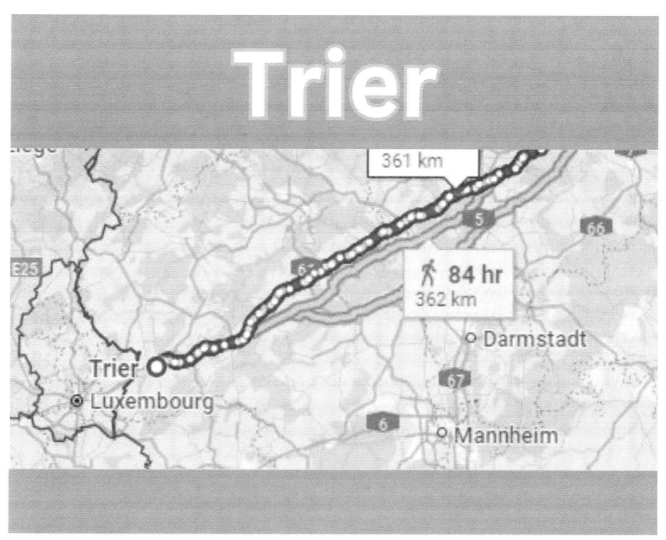

SCAN HERE

HOW TO USE QR CODE

- Open your phone's camera app or download scanner app from play store or apple store
- Point the camera at the QR code for a few seconds (no need to take a photo).
- A link should appear on the display, leading you to the location of the code

Moselle Valley

Munich

SCAN HERE

HOW TO USE QR CODE

- Open your phone's camera app or download scanner app from play store or apple store
- Point the camera at the QR code for a few seconds (no need to take a photo).
- A link should appear on the display, leading you to the location of the code

Neuschwanstein Castle

Bavarian Alps

Porsche Museum

Black Forest

Lindau

SCAN HERE

HOW TO USE QR CODE

- Open your phone's camera app or download scanner app from play store or apple store
- Point the camera at the QR code for a few seconds (no need to take a photo).
- A link should appear on the display, leading you to the location of the code

Reichenau Island

Chapter 3

Scenic Road Trips & Themed Routes

Germany is a dream destination for road trips, offering well-maintained roads, breathtaking landscapes, and historic landmarks along the way. Whether you're looking for medieval castles, scenic vineyards, coastal escapes, or fairy-tale towns, these themed routes take you through the country's most picturesque regions.

Each of these road trips provides a unique experience, allowing travelers to immerse themselves in history, culture, and natural beauty while enjoying Germany's world-famous highways.

A Journey through Medieval Towns and Fairytale Castles

Distance: ~350 km (217 miles)

Route: Würzburg → Rothenburg ob der Tauber → Augsburg → Füssen

The Romantic Road is Germany's most famous scenic route, winding through storybook villages, rolling vineyards, and centuries old castles. This drive is perfect for those who love history, architecture, and traditional German culture.

Highlights Along the Route

1. Würzburg: Start in this beautiful baroque city famous for the Würzburg Residence (UNESCO World Heritage Site) and its vineyards along the Main River.

2. Rothenburg ob der Tauber: A medieval town frozen in time with cobblestone streets, half timbered houses, and the famous Christmas Village.

3. Augsburg: Is the one of Germany oldest cities known for Renaissance architecture and the historic Fuggerei Europe's oldest social housing complex.

4. Neuschwanstein Castle: The crown jewel of the Romantic Road, this fairy-tale castle inspired Disney's Cinderella Castle.

Best for: Couples, history lovers, and anyone look for an old world European experience.

Panoramic Mountain Landscapes from Lake Constance to Berchtesgaden

Distance: ~450 km (280 miles)

Route: Lindau → Garmisch-Partenkirchen → Zugspitze → Berchtesgaden

The German Alpine Road (Deutsche Alpenstraße) is a breathtaking drive through the Bavarian Alps, featuring snow-capped peaks, crystal-clear lakes, and charming alpine villages.

Highlights Along the Route:

Lindau: A picturesque island town on Lake Constance with panoramic views of the Alps.

Garmisch-Partenkirchen: A charming Bavarian ski town, home to Germany highest mountain, Zugspitze (2,962m).

Berchtesgaden & Königssee: One of Germany most scenic lakes, surrounded by dramatic alpine cliffs.

The Berchtesgaden National Park: A Natural Wonderland National Park, a gem of unspoiled nature. This spectacular region is renowned for its dramatic cliffs dense forests, and crystal-clear lakes, particularly the famous Königssee. The park is a sanctuary for diverse wildlife and offers myriad trails that lead to breathtaking viewpoints, including the famous Eagle's Nest, which perches dramatically above the town of Berchtesgaden and serves as a historical site. The landscape here is characterized by rugged terrain, hidden waterfalls, and lush valleys that evoke a sense of peace and adventure.

Best for: Nature lovers, adventure seekers, and photographers.

Exploring Germany's Best Vineyards Along the Moselle and Rhine Rivers

Distance: ~170 km (105 miles)

Route: Trier → Bernkastel-Kues → Cochem → Rüdesheim

Germany's wine-growing regions produce some of the best Riesling in the world, and this scenic drive along the Moselle and Rhine Rivers offers stunning landscapes, charming villages, and vineyard-covered hills.

Highlights Along the Route

1. Trier: Germany oldest city, featuring Roman ruins and a historic wine culture.

2. Bernkastel-Kues: A charming village with half timbered houses and riverside wineries.

3. Cochem Castle: A hilltop fortress overlooking the Moselle River.

4. Rüdesheim am Rhein: A UNESCO listed wine town, famous for the Drosselgasse wine taverns.

Best for: Wine enthusiasts, food lovers, and those looking for a relaxed countryside drive.

Brothers Grimm's Legacy Through Forests and Historic Towns

Distance: ~600 km (373 miles)

Route: Hanau → Kassel → Sababurg → Bremen

The German Fairy Tale Route takes you through forests, castles, and villages that inspired the famous fairy tales of the Brothers Grimm, including Snow White, Sleeping Beauty, and Little Red Riding Hood.

Highlights Along the Route:

1. **Hanau:** The birthplace of the Brothers Grimm and home to the Fairy Tale Festival.

2. **Kassel & Grimmwelt Museum:** A museum dedicated to the Grimm brothers' stories.

3. **Sababurg (Sleeping Beauty Castle):** The inspiration for Sleeping Beauty's castle nestled in the Reinhardswald Forest.

4. **Bremen:** The final stop, famous for the Bremen Town Musicians statue, inspired by the Grimm fairy tale.

Best for: Families, literature lovers, and fairy-tale enthusiasts.

Exploring Germany's Grand Fortresses from Heidelberg to Bavaria

Distance: ~1,200 km (746 miles)

Route: Mannheim → Heidelberg → Nuremberg → Neuschwanstein

Germany is home to more than 20,000 castles, and this epic road trip takes you through some of the most iconic and well-preserved fortresses.

Highlights Along the Route:

1. **Heidelberg Castle:** Overlooking the Neckar River, this is a romantic ruin with a rich history.

2. **Nuremberg Castle:** A medieval fortress with stunning views over the city.

3. **Hohenzollern Castle:** A storybook castle perched high on a hill, home to German royalty.

4. **Neuschwanstein Castle:** The most famous castle in Germany with breathtaking views of the Bavarian Alps.

Best for: History buffs, photographers, and architecture lovers.

A Coastal Drive Through Charming Seaside Towns and Nature Parks

Distance: ~700 km (435 miles)

Route: Lübeck → Rostock → Rügen Island → Usedom

Germany's Baltic Sea coastline is filled with seaside resorts, white-sand beaches, and historic port cities. This coastal drive offers a blend of nature, history, and relaxation.

Highlights Along the Route

1. Lübeck: A UNESCO-listed hanseatic town with medieval architecture.

2. Rostock & Warnemünde: A lively port city with beautiful beaches.

3. Rügen Island: Known for the white chalk cliffs of Jasmund National Park.

4. Usedom Island: A charming beach destination with classic German seaside resorts.

Best for: Beach lovers, nature enthusiasts, and those seeking a relaxed coastal escape.

The Ultimate Road Trip Experience

Germany's scenic routes offer something for every traveler, from fairy-tale castles to alpine adventures and coastal getaways. Whether you prefer cultural road trips, wine-tasting journeys, or breathtaking mountain drives, each of these themed routes provides an unforgettable experience.

The ultimate road trip experience in Germany is about more than just the destinations; it's about the journey and the connections you make along the way. By carefully choosing your route, embracing the culinary delights, and cherishing the moments of spontaneity, you'll create a mosaic of memories that lasts a lifetime.

Würzburg

SCAN HERE

HOW TO USE QR CODE

- Open your phone's camera app or download scanner app from play store or apple store
- Point the camera at the QR code for a few seconds (no need to take a photo).
- A link should appear on the display, leading you to the location of the code

Rothenburg ob der Tauber

Augsburg

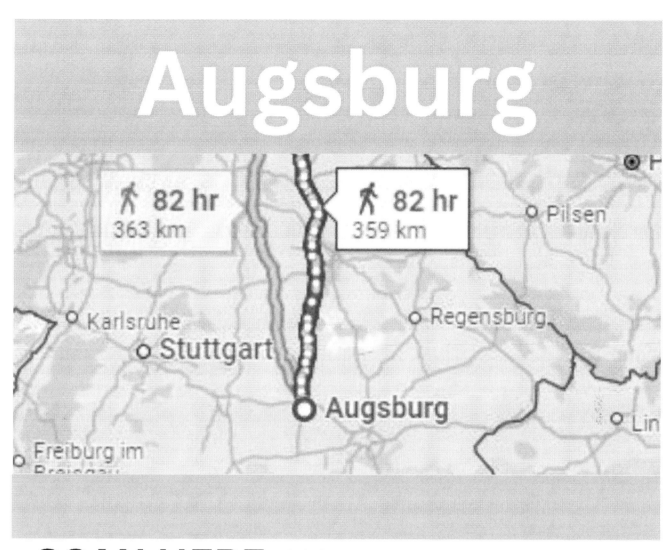

SCAN HERE

HOW TO USE QR CODE

- Open your phone's camera app or download scanner app from play store or apple store
- Point the camera at the QR code for a few seconds (no need to take a photo).
- A link should appear on the display, leading you to the location of the code

Garmisch
Partenkirchen

Berchtesgaden

SCAN HERE

HOW TO USE QR CODE

- Open your phone's camera app or download scanner app from play store or apple store
- Point the camera at the QR code for a few seconds (no need to take a photo).
- A link should appear on the display, leading you to the location of the code

Zugspitze

Königssee

Bernkastel-Kues

Cochem Castle

Rüdesheim am Rhein

Hanau

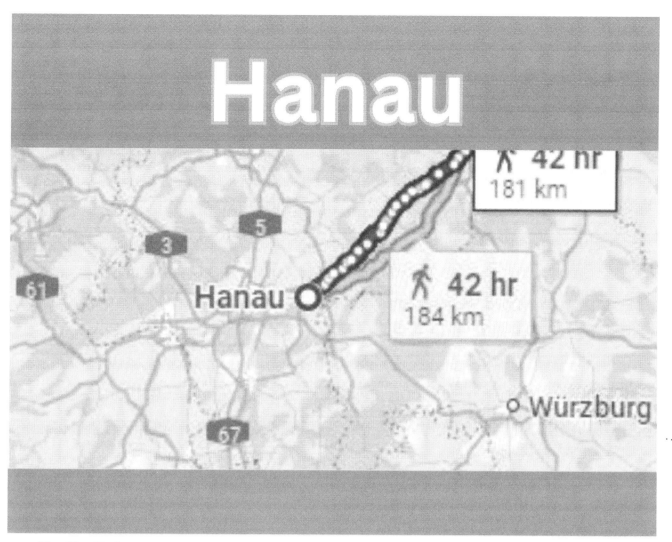

SCAN HERE

HOW TO USE QR CODE

- Open your phone's camera app or download scanner app from play store or apple store
- Point the camera at the QR code for a few seconds (no need to take a photo).
- A link should appear on the display, leading you to the location of the code

Kassel

SCAN HERE

HOW TO USE QR CODE

- Open your phone's camera app or download scanner app from play store or apple store
- Point the camera at the QR code for a few seconds (no need to take a photo).
- A link should appear on the display, leading you to the location of the code

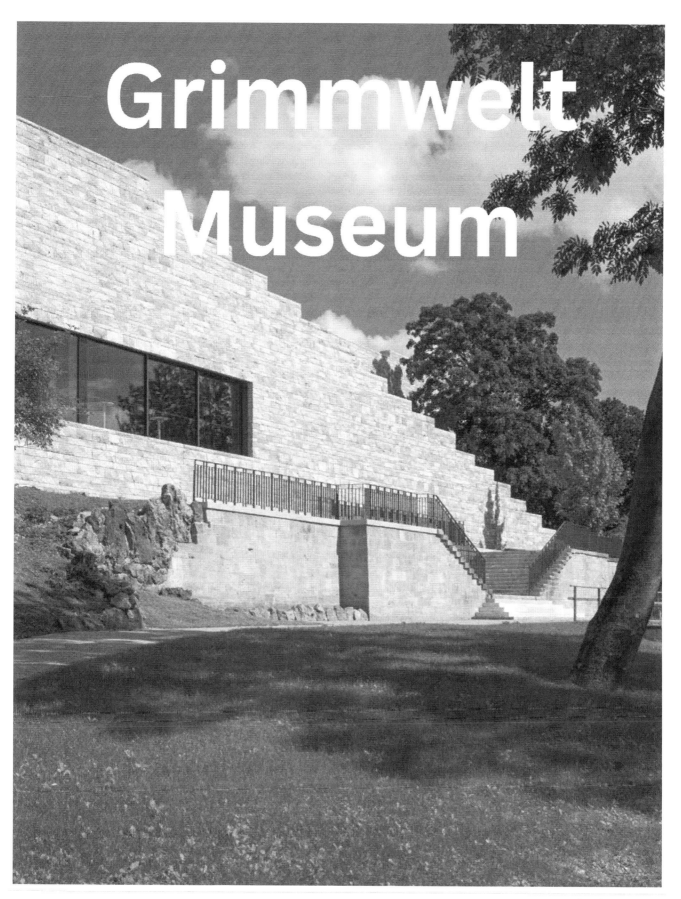

Grimmwelt Museum

Sleeping Beauty Castle Sababurg

Mannheim

266 km

SCAN HERE

HOW TO USE QR CODE

- Open your phone's camera app or download scanner app from play store or apple store
- Point the camera at the QR code for a few seconds (no need to take a photo).
- A link should appear on the display, leading you to the location of the code

Heidelberg

SCAN HERE

HOW TO USE QR CODE

- Open your phone's camera app or download scanner app from play store or apple store
- Point the camera at the QR code for a few seconds (no need to take a photo).
- A link should appear on the display, leading you to the location of the code

Heidelberg Castle

Nuremberg Castle

Hohenzollern Castle

Rügen Island

Usedom Island

Chapter 4

Germany's Road System & Navigation Tips

Germany is known for having one of the most efficient and well-maintained road networks in the world. From the high-speed Autobahn to scenic country roads, driving in Germany is an adventure that combines smooth highways, breathtaking landscapes, and well-marked routes. To make the most of your road trip through Germany, it's essential to understand the country's driving laws, rental options, road signs, and seasonal considerations. Here are the practical tips to ensure a smooth and enjoyable driving experience.

Understanding the Autobahn

Speed Limits, Etiquette, and Toll-Free Driving

The Autobahn is Germany's famous federal highway system, known for its high speeds and lack of a general speed limit on certain sections. However, driving on the Autobahn comes with its own rules and etiquette.

Key Features of the Autobahn

1. No General Speed Limit: While some sections of the Autobahn have no official speed limit, a recommended speed of 130 km/h (80 mph) is advised.

2. Speed Limits in Certain Areas: Urban zones, construction sites, and accident-prone areas have speed limits between 80-120 km/h (50-75 mph).

3. Right Lane Rule: The left lane is strictly for overtaking. After passing, you must return to the right lane to avoid blocking traffic.

4. No Toll Fees: Unlike many European highways, the Autobahn is free for private vehicles, except for trucks over 7.5 tons, which pay a toll.

5. No Stopping Allowed: Stopping on the Autobahn is illegal unless there is an emergency. Running out of fuel is considered driver negligence, so always fill up before long drives.

Tip: Always be aware of fast-moving vehicles in the left lane, especially sports cars and high-performance vehicles traveling at speeds over 200 km/h (125 mph).

Driving Laws & Regulations 2025 Update

Before driving in Germany, it's important to know the latest traffic laws and regulations.

Speed Limits (2025 Regulations)

Urban areas: 50 km/h (31 mph) unless otherwise posted.

Rural roads: 100 km/h (62 mph).

Autobahn (recommended): 130 km/h (80 mph), but no strict limit unless posted.

Emissions Zones & Environmental Stickers (Umweltplakette)

Many German cities have low emission zones (Umweltzonen) to reduce pollution.

Green Sticker Required: To enter low mission zones in cities (Berlin, Munich, Stuttgart, etc.), cars must display a green environmental sticker.

Fines: Driving in these areas without a sticker results in a €80+ fine.

Required Documents for Driving in Germany

Valid Driver's License: EU citizens can use their national licenses; non-EU drivers may need an International Driving Permit (IDP).

Vehicle Registration & Insurance: If renting a car, ensure the rental agency provides proof of registration and insurance.

Safety Equipment in Car: By law, all vehicles must carry.

- A reflective safety vest
- A warning triangle
- A first-aid kit

Tip: Always check local rules before entering a city as some may have stricter emission requirements.

Renting a Car in Germany

Insurance, Rental Agencies, & Best Car Types for Travel

Renting a car is a great way to explore Germany but choosing the right vehicle and insurance is key.

Top Rental Agencies in Germany

Sixt: A German company with competitive prices.

Europcar: This Company offers a wide selection of vehicles.

Hertz & Avis: International companies with locations across Germany.

Best Car Types for Travel

Compact Cars (VW Golf, Audi A3): Best for city driving and fuel efficiency.

SUVs & Crossovers (BMW X3, Volkswagen Tiguan): Ideal for family trips and winter travel.

Luxury & Sports Cars (Porsche, Mercedes Benz): Perfect for Autobahn enthusiasts.

Insurance Considerations

Basic Insurance (included): This covers liability for damages to others but not your own car.

Collision Damage Waiver (CDW): This reduces your financial responsibility if the car is damaged.

Full Coverage Insurance: This is the Best option for stress-free travel.

Tip: Many rental agencies require a credit card deposit, so check your card's rental coverage before booking.

Road Signs & Symbols

Common German Road Signs and Their Meanings

Germany's road signs are straightforward, but some might be unfamiliar to foreign drivers.

Important Signs to Know

Red Circle Signs: Indicate prohibitions (e.g. no entry, no parking, and speed limits).

Blue Signs: Provide mandatory instructions (e.g., keep right, bus lanes, one-way streets).

Triangle Signs: Warn of hazards (e.g., sharp curves, pedestrian crossings, wildlife zones).

Tip: Always pay attention to roundabouts and priority signs, as German roads often have right-of-way rules at intersections.

Fueling & Charging Stations

Where to Find Gas Stations & EV Charging Points

Germany has an extensive network of fueling and charging stations.

Finding Gas Stations

Autobahn Service Stations: These are Open 24/7, but prices are higher than in cities.

City & Village Stations: Cheaper fuel, but May close at 10 PM or earlier.

Electric Vehicle Charging

Fast-Charging Stations: These are available at service stations, shopping centers, and city parking lots.

Charging Networks: Major providers include, IONITY, EnBW and Tesla Superchargers.

Tip: Gasoline and diesel prices fluctuate daily, so use apps like Clever Tanken to find the cheapest fuel.

Snow Tires, Chains, & Driving Safely in Alpine Regions

Driving in winter conditions can present unique challenges, especially in Germany, where snow, ice, and freezing temperatures are common from November to March. Understanding and adhering to winter driving rules is crucial for ensuring safety on the roads.

Winter Driving Rules in Germany

Winter Tires: It is mandatory to have winter tires (M+S or 3PMSF marked) from October to Easter when conditions require it. These tires provide better traction on snow and ice.

Fluid Levels: Make sure your windshield washer fluid is suitable for low temperatures and that engine coolant is at the right level to prevent freezing.

Snow Chains: Required in mountainous areas; look for signs indicating when chains must be used.

Black Ice Warning (Glatteis): Be cautious of hidden ice patches, especially in shaded areas and bridges.

Battery Check: Cold weather can be tough on batteries. Ensure your battery is in good condition.

Emergency Kit: Carry an emergency kit that includes blankets, food, water, a flashlight, and basic tools.

Reduced Speed: Drive slower than usual to maintain better control. Ice can form on the road unexpectedly, especially on bridges and shaded areas.

Tip: If driving in Bavaria or the Black Forest, rent a 4WD vehicle for better handling on snow-covered roads.

Navigating Germany with Confidence

With its efficient road network, scenic routes, and world-famous Autobahn, Germany is a fantastic destination for road trips. By understanding driving laws, road signs, and rental car options, you can enjoy a safe and hassle-free journey.

IONITY Charging Station

Chapter 5

Navigating Cities & Urban Transport

Germany cities are known for their efficient public transportation, pedestrian friendly streets, and well planned infrastructure, making it easy for both residents and tourists to get around. While driving in the countryside and along scenic routes is a joy, navigating urban areas requires a different approach.

This section will guide you through the best ways to explore German cities, from public transport options and bike rentals to parking strategies and rideshare alternatives.

Best Ways to Get Around Cities

Germany's major cities Berlin, Munich, Hamburg, Frankfurt, and Cologne boast some of the most efficient public transport systems in Europe. Depending on the city, you can get around using it.

1. Public Transport (U-Bahn, S-Bahn, Trams & Buses)

U-Bahn (Underground Metro): Found in larger cities like Berlin, Munich, Hamburg, and Frankfurt, offering fast and frequent connections.

S-Bahn (Suburban Rail): Connects city centers with suburbs and is often used for airport transfers.

Trams (Straßenbahn): These are Available in cities like Dresden, Stuttgart, and Leipzig, providing a scenic and convenient way to travel.

Buses: Fill in gaps where metro and tram lines don't reach, especially in smaller cities and rural areas.

Tip: Buy a day pass or a weekly ticket for unlimited travel within a city this is cheaper than single tickets if using transport multiple times a day.

2. Bike Rentals & E-Scooters

Germany is one of the most bike-friendly countries in Europe, with dedicated bike lanes and bike-sharing programs in almost every city.

Popular bike rental services

Call a Bike (by Deutsche Bahn) Available in major cities.

Nextbike: Covers smaller towns and tourist areas.

 E-scooter rentals (Great for short distances):

Tier, Lime, Voi and Bolt operate in Berlin, Munich, Cologne, and other cities.

Tip: Bike lanes are often separate from pedestrian paths, so be mindful of designated cycling areas to avoid fines.

3. Pedestrian-Friendly Zones

Most German city centers are designed for walking, making it easy to explore historic districts, shopping streets, and riverside promenades on foot.

Famous pedestrian zones include

- Berlin: Unter den Linden, Kurfürstendamm.
- Munich: Marienplatz, Viktualienmarkt.
- Hamburg: Jungfernstieg, Speicherstadt.
- Frankfurt: Römerberg, Zeil shopping street.

Tip: Many cities offer guided walking tours, which are a great way to learn about the history and culture while strolling through charming streets.

Parking Options for City Visits & Avoiding Congestion Zones

Germany's Park & Ride (P+R) system is an excellent option for visitors who want to avoid city center traffic and expensive parking fees.

How Park & Ride Works

Drive to a P+R lot on the outskirts of a city.

Take public transport into the city center (U-Bahn, S-Bahn, or tram). Cheaper than city parking many are free or cost only a few euros.

Best Cities for Park & Ride

Berlin: Over 40 P+R locations linked to the S-Bahn.

Munich: Parking is available near major U-Bahn stations.

Hamburg: Well-connected with S-Bahn and U-Bahn services.

Frankfurt: is ideal for avoiding busy business districts.

Tip: Many Park & Ride stations have EV charging points, making them a great option for electric vehicle drivers.

Driving in Historic Towns Traffic Restrictions, Permits, & Car-Free Zones

Many old towns and historic districts in Germany have strict driving restrictions to preserve their charm and reduce pollution.

Types of Driving Restrictions

Car-Free Zones (Fußgängerzone): Completely closed to vehicles, except for residents and deliveries (e.g., Munich's Marienplatz, Old Bridge Heidelberg).
Limited Access Areas: Some historic districts allow cars but require a special permit (e.g., Rothenburg ob der Tauber).

Underground Parking Garages: Many towns have hidden parking lots just outside the historic center (e.g., Regensburg, Bamberg).

Tip: Always check whether your destination requires an emissions sticker (Umweltplakette) before driving into the city.

Uber Alternatives & Official Taxi Regulations

While Uber is available in Germany, it is not as widely used as it is in the US or the UK. Instead, Germany has regulated taxi services and local rideshare alternatives.

Taxis in Germany

Official taxis are beige-colored with a TAXI sign on top.

Fare is regulated meters start at around €4, then €2 per km. It can be hailed on the street, found at taxi stands, or booked via apps.

Popular Taxi Apps

FreeNow (formerly MyTaxi): This is the most widely used.

Taxi.eu: This covers smaller cities and towns.

Rideshare & Carpooling Options:

Uber: Available in Berlin, Munich, Frankfurt, and Düsseldorf.

Bolt: This service offers lower fares than taxis.

BlaBlaCar: A long distance carpooling service, great for budget friendly intercity travel.

Tip: Many German still prefer taxis over Uber especially for airport transfers.

How to Combine Road Trips with Germany's Rail & Bus Networks

Germany's rail and bus networks make it easy to combine city travel with scenic road trips.

1. Deutsche Bahn (DB): Germany's National Rail System

Best for long-distance travel between major cities.

Regional Passes (e.g., Bayern Ticket) offer unlimited travel in a region for a day.

ICE high-speed trains connect Berlin, Munich, Frankfurt, and Hamburg in less than 4 hours.

2. Intercity & Regional Buses

FlixBus: Cheap and reliable, FlixBus connects cities and even neighboring countries.

3. Deutsche Bahn Buses: Complements train routes for areas without direct rail connections.

Tip: If traveling by car, use a train+car combo like DB Autozug (car-carrying train) for long-distance routes.

Whether you're navigating big cities, renting a bike, using Park & Ride, or hopping on a train, Germany offers a range of efficient transport options. With a little planning, you can seamlessly explore urban centers without the hassle of traffic or parking problems.

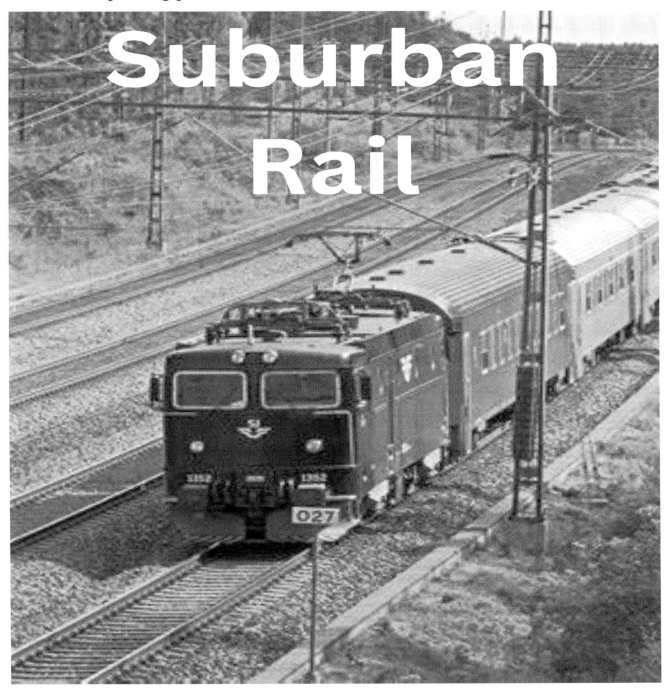

Unter den Linden

Kurfürstendamm

Marienplatz

S-Bahn

Old Bridge
Heidelberg

Regensburg

SCAN HERE

HOW TO USE QR CODE

- Open your phone's camera app or download scanner app from play store or apple store
- Point the camera at the QR code for a few seconds (no need to take a photo).
- A link should appear on the display, leading you to the location of the code

Bamberg

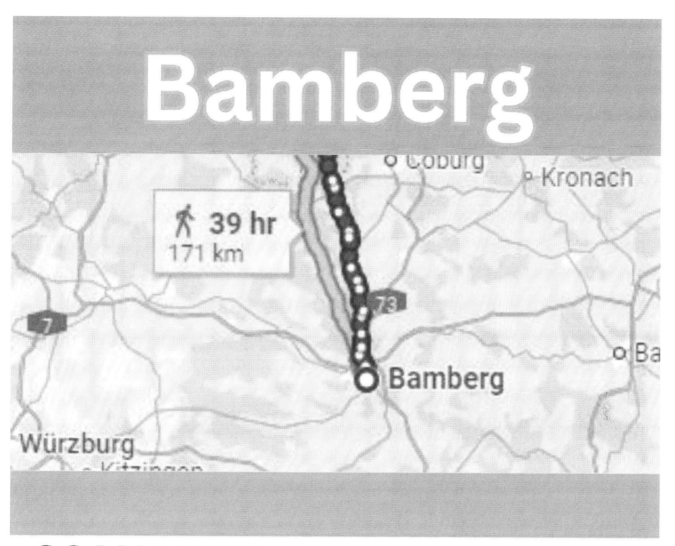

SCAN HERE

HOW TO USE QR CODE

- Open your phone's camera app or download scanner app from play store or apple store
- Point the camera at the QR code for a few seconds (no need to take a photo).
- A link should appear on the display, leading you to the location of the code

Chapter 6

Accommodation & Roadside Services

Germany offers a wide range of accommodation options for travelers, from luxury hotels in major cities to quaint guesthouses in small villages and campsites for those who love the outdoors. Whether you're road-tripping across the country or stopping for a quick overnight stay, understanding where to stay and what roadside services are available will make your journey much more enjoyable.

These are the best places to stay, camping options, rest stops on the Autobahn, and top roadside dining experiences.

Hotels & Guesthouses

Germany offers a diverse selection of hotels and guesthouses, catering to all types of travelers from those seeking luxury experiences to budget-conscious road-trippers.

1. Types of Accommodation in Germany

Hotels: Found in cities, towns, and tourist hotspots. Options range from 5-star luxury stays to budget-friendly chains like B&B Hotels, Motel One, and Ibis.

Guesthouses Gasthäuser & Pensionen: Family run charming, and affordable lodgings, perfect for a more authentic experience in smaller towns and countryside areas.

Hostels: A great budget option, especially in Berlin, Munich, Hamburg, and Cologne. Look for A&O Hostels, Meininger, and Generator Hostels.

Roadside Motels & Budget Hotels: Ideal for road-trippers looking for a quick and affordable overnight stay along highways.

2. Best Locations for Staying Overnight

City Centers: If you want to explore on foot, staying in central districts (e.g., Berlin Mitte, Munich Altstadt) is best.

Near Highways (Autobahnhotels): Convenient for travelers on long drives, with options like Autobahn hotels, Ibis Budget, and B&B Hotels.

Scenic Countryside Inns: Great for those seeking a peaceful retreat in regions like Bavaria or the Black Forest.

3. Booking Tips for the Best Deals

Use hotel comparison websites like Booking.com, Trivago, and Expedia to find the best prices.

Book in advance if traveling during peak seasons (e.g., Oktoberfest in Munich, Christmas Markets in December).

Look for special road trip-friendly hotels with free parking and breakfast included.

Germany's Best Campsites, Motorhome Parks & Campervan Tips

Camping and RV travel are popular and well-organized in Germany, with hundreds of campsites and motorhome parks across the country.

1. Top Campsites & Motorhome Parks

Best Camping Destinations

Black Forest (Schwarzwald): Stunning nature with well-equipped campsites.

Bavarian Alps: Campsites near Neuschwanstein Castle and Zugspitze.

Lake Constance (Bodensee): Scenic lakeside camping with great facilities.

Baltic Sea & North Sea Coasts: Beautiful beaches with dedicated RV parks.

Motorhome & Campervan Sites (Stellplätze)

Reisemobilhafen Twistesee: Designated spots for motorhomes with electricity water, and waste disposal.

Wohnmobilhafen: Larger motorhome parks with additional amenities like showers and restaurants.

2. Campervan Travel Tips

Wild camping is restricted: Unlike in some countries, wild camping is not allowed in Germany except in designated areas.

Use camping apps: Apps like Park4Night and Campercontact help find the best overnight spots.

Renting a campervan? Check out McRent, Indie Campers, or Yescapa for reliable campervan rentals.

Highway Rest Stops & Services

Germany's Autobahn has excellent roadside facilities to ensure a comfortable journey for drivers.

1. Types of Rest Stops (Raststätten & Parkplätze)

Raststätte (Full-Service Rest Areas): Located along the Autobahn, offering.

- Toilets & showers
- Restaurants & cafés
- Shops & fuel stations

Parkplatz (Basic Parking Areas) – Simple rest stops with:

- Parking spaces
- Basic toilets (some may require a small fee)

EV Charging Stations: Germany has an extensive network of fast charging station with IONITY, EnBW, and Tesla Superchargers along major highways.

2. Best Autobahn Rest Stops

Rasthof Medenbach (A3, Frankfurt-Cologne): Excellent facilities with a restaurant, clean restrooms, and a fuel station.

Serways Tank & Rast (A9, Berlin-Munich): One of Germany's best rest areas with multiple dining options.

Raststätte Allgäuer Tor (A7, Bavaria): This offers great Alpine views and a local food market.

Tip: Use "Autohof" rest stops (located slightly off the Autobahn) for cheaper food and fuel prices compared to directly on the highway.

Best Roadside Restaurants, Regional Dishes, & Must-Try Food

Germany is famous for its regional cuisine, and road-trippers have plenty of opportunities to sample delicious local specialties.

1. Best Roadside Restaurants & Local Dining Spots

Serways Restaurants: Common along the Autobahn, offering traditional German meals like Schnitzel and Bratwurst.

Hofbräuhaus-style Beer Gardens: Found near highways, serving authentic Bavarian food.

Raststätte Restaurants (Burger King, Nordsee, Vapiano): Found at major Autobahn rest areas.

2. Must-Try Dishes While Traveling

Currywurst: Germany's famous sausage with curry ketchup and fries (best found in Berlin rest stops).

Brezn (Pretzels): A Bavarian road-trip classic, often sold at bakeries in service stations.

Schweinebraten (Roast Pork): A hearty meal available at Autohof and local restaurants.

Rye Bread Sandwiches (Belegte Brötchen): Great for a quick breakfast or snack at highway bakeries.

Black Forest Cake (Schwarzwälder Kirschtorte): A must-try if traveling through southern Germany.

Tip: Try "Rasthof" rest stops instead of fast food chains for a more authentic and local food experience.

Whether you're staying in a hotel, guesthouse, or campsite, Germany offers plenty of comfortable and convenient options for travelers. Combine this with well-equipped Autobahn rest stops and delicious roadside food, and your journey through Germany will be both enjoyable and hassle-free.

Berlin Mitte

Autobahn hotels

B&B Hotel

Bavaria

SCAN HERE

HOW TO USE QR CODE

- Open your phone's camera app or download scanner app from play store or apple store
- Point the camera at the QR code for a few seconds (no need to take a photo).
- A link should appear on the display, leading you to the location of the code

Black Forest

Bavarian Alps

Reisemobilhafen
Twistesee

Tank & Rast
Raststätte

Chapter 7

Outdoor Adventures & Nature Escapes

Germany is a paradise for nature lovers, offering breathtaking landscapes, well-maintained hiking and cycling routes, pristine lakes and rivers, and top-notch skiing resorts. Beyond its famous cities, the country is home to enchanting forests, charming villages, and relaxing spa towns, making it an ideal destination for outdoor adventures and hidden getaways.

These are best national parks to explore in Germany's, cycling routes, water activities, ski destinations, and wellness retreats, along with lesser-known villages, regional festivals, and must-try culinary delights.

Hiking & National Parks

Germany's diverse landscapes make it a hiker's dream destination, with well-marked trails ranging from gentle forest walks to challenging mountain hikes.

1. Top Hiking Destinations in Germany

The Black Forest (Schwarzwald): A fairytale-like region with dense forests, rolling hills, and traditional villages. Famous trails include:

Westweg Trail (285 km): A long-distance trek from Pforzheim to Basel.

Triberg Waterfalls Trail: A short hike to Germany's highest waterfalls.

Harz Mountains: A mystical region known for rugged peaks, medieval towns, and legends of witches. Best hikes:

Brocken Summit Trail: Climb to the highest peak (1,141m) with stunning views.

Harzer Hexenstieg: A 100 km legendary trail through forests and cliffs.

Saxon Switzerland National Park: A unique hiking paradise with sandstone rock formations and dramatic cliffs near Dresden.

Must-see

Bastei Bridge Trail: One of Germany's most iconic viewpoints.

Schrammsteine Ridge: A thrilling hike with panoramic views.

Bavarian Forest National Park: Germany's oldest national park, featuring:

Rachelsee Trail: A scenic hike to an alpine lake.

Tree Top Walk Baumwipfelpfad: An elevated walkway offering breathtaking forest views.

2. Hiking Tips for Travelers

Wear proper hiking shoes: Many trails have uneven terrain.

Check weather conditions: Some mountain paths can be slippery after rain.

Use Germany's well-marked trails: Sign posted routes make navigation easy.

Cycling Routes: EuroVelo Paths, Scenic Countryside Rides, & City Bike Lanes

Germany is one of Europe most bike friendly countries, with well maintained cycling paths that pass through cities, forests, and picturesque countryside.

3. Top Cycling Routes in Germany

EuroVelo 6 (Danube Cycle Path): A legendary long-distance route passing through Bavaria along the Danube River, perfect for scenic countryside rides.

Berlin Copenhagen Cycle Route: A historic and nature filled route connecting Berlin with Denmark, passing through lakes and forests.

Romantic Road Cycle Route: A charming ride through medieval villages, castles, and vineyards, including Rothenburg ob der Tauber.

Elbe River Cycle Path: A relaxed ride along the Elbe River, passing through Dresden, Hamburg, and Saxon Switzerland.

City Bike Lanes: Most German cities have dedicated bike lanes, with bike rentals available in Berlin, Munich, and Hamburg.

Tip: Use bike rental apps like Call a Bike, Nextbike, or Lime for easy access to bicycles in cities.

Lakes & Rivers

Germany boasts stunning lakes and rivers perfect for boating, swimming, and relaxing nature escapes.

1.1 Most Beautiful Lakes & Water Destinations

1. Lake Königssee (Bavaria): A crystal clear alpine lake surrounded by majestic mountains. Take a boat trip to St. Bartholomew's Church.

2. Lake Constance (Bodensee): Shared with Switzerland and Austria, this is Germany's largest lake, ideal for sailing, cycling, and wine tasting.

3. Eibsee (Bavaria): A turquoise-blue lake at the base of Germany's highest peak, Zugspitze perfect for kayaking and photography.

4. The Rhine River: A scenic river cruise offers views of medieval castles and vineyards along the Rhine Valley.

5. The Spreewald Biosphere Reserve: A unique water landscape near Berlin with traditional wooden boat tours through canals.

Tip: Many lakes have dedicated swimming areas with clear waters and sandy beaches, especially in Bavaria and Brandenburg.

Skiing & Winter Sports

Germany is an excellent winter sports destination, with ski resorts and cross-country trails across the Bavarian Alps, Harz Mountains, and Thuringian Forest.

2.1 Top Ski Resorts in Germany

1. Garmisch-Partenkirchen (Bavaria): Germany's most famous ski resort, home to the Zugspitze Glacier with world-class slopes.

2. Oberstdorf Kleinwalsertal (Allgäu): A family friendly ski area with excellent snow conditions.

3. Braunlage (Harz Mountains): A great option for beginners, located in northern Germany.

4. Feldberg (Black Forest): The highest peak in southwest Germany, offering ski and snowboard trails.

Tip: Germany's ski resorts have affordable ski passes compared to Austria or Switzerland.

Germany's Historic Thermal Baths & Relaxation Retreats

Germany has a long tradition of wellness and spa culture, with many thermal baths, hot springs, and luxurious spa resorts.

1.1 Best Spa Towns in Germany

1. Baden-Baden (Black Forest): A world-famous spa town with luxurious thermal baths likes Caracalla Spa and Friedrichsbad.

2. Bad Wörishofen (Bavaria): The birthplace of Kneipp therapy, known for its healing water treatments.

3. Bad Ems (Rhine Valley): A historic thermal spa town with scenic river views.

Tip: Many spa towns offer day passes, so you can relax in thermal pools after a long drive.

Hidden Gems & Local Experiences

1. Charming Villages to Visit

Rothenburg ob der Tauber: A storybook medieval town with half-timbered houses and cobblestone streets.

Monschau (Eifel): A picturesque village with scenic hiking trails and historic mills.

Meersburg (Lake Constance): A lakeside town with a beautiful castle and wine-tasting spots.

2. Underrated Destinations

Görlitz: A stunning border town with Polish influences.

Bamberg: A UNESCO-listed town with a medieval atmosphere and smoked beer (Rauchbier).

3. Local Festivals & Events

Oktoberfest (Munich): One of the world most famous festivals, Oktoberfest, takes place in Munich from late September to the first weekend in October. This 16- to 18-day festival attracts millions of visitors who come to enjoy traditional Bavarian beer, regional foods, and live music in enormous beer tents.

Christkindlmarkt (Nuremberg): The Nuremberg Christkindlmarkt, held from late November to Christmas Eve, is one of Germany's oldest and most famous Christmas markets. Visitors can enjoy a festive atmosphere with beautifully crafted ornaments, delicious gingerbread, and local delicacies such as bratwurst and mulled wine, all amidst stunning medieval architecture.

Christmas Traditions: Throughout Germany, the Advent season is marked with festive markets, concerts, and local customs. Each town and city has its own unique way of celebrating Christmas, from lighting ceremonies to Advent wreath displays, making the holiday season a magical time to experience German culture.

Documenta (Kassel): Held every five years, Documenta is one of the most important international exhibitions of contemporary art.

4. Culinary Specialties by Region

Bavaria: Pretzels, Weisswurst, and Schweinshaxe.

Rhine Valley: Riesling wine and Flammkuchen.

Northern Germany: Fresh seafood and Fischbrötchen (fish sandwiches).

From mountain adventures to spa retreats and charming villages, Germany offers endless outdoor experiences. Whether you're hiking, cycling, skiing, or indulging in local food and festivals, this country is a treasure trove of natural wonders and cultural delights.

Berlin Mitte

Triberg Waterfalls

Brocken Summit

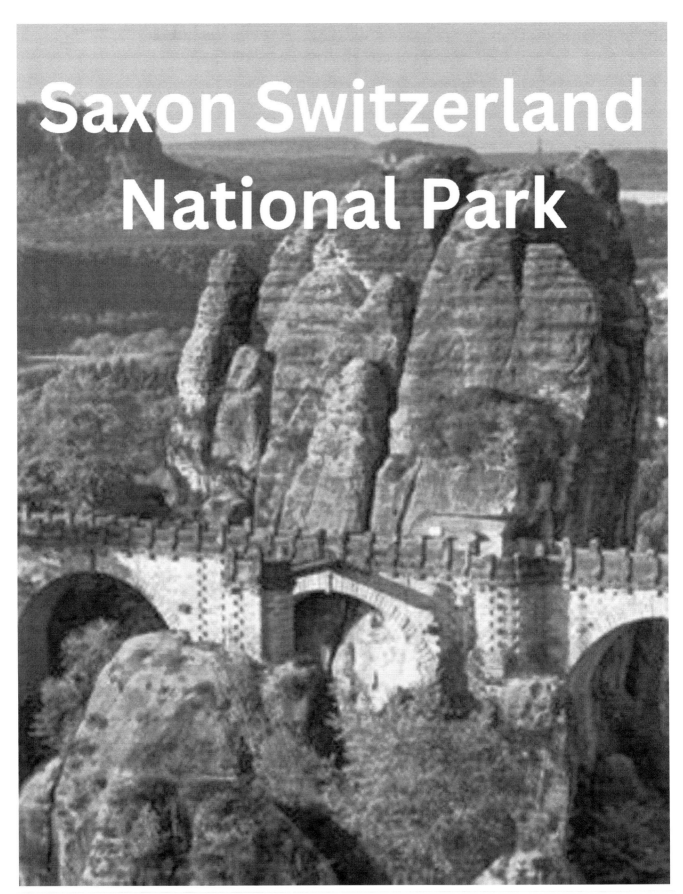

Saxon Switzerland National Park

Bastei Bridge

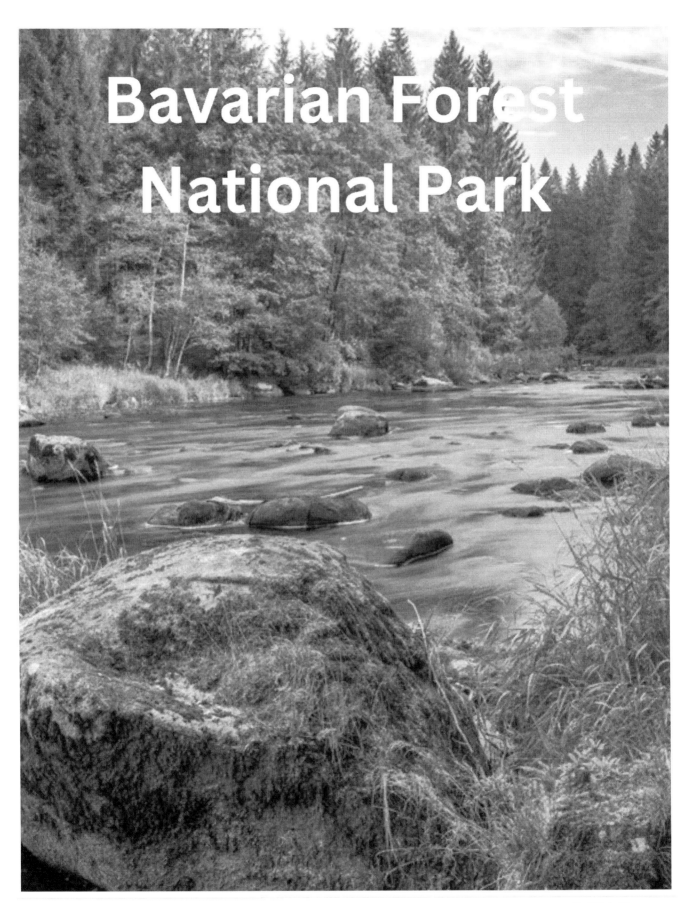

Bavarian Forest National Park

Rachelsee

Danube River

Elbe River

Königssee

Eibsee

Rhine River

Garmisch-Partenkirchen

Feldberg

Bad Wörishofen

SCAN HERE

HOW TO USE QR CODE

- Open your phone's camera app or download scanner app from play store or apple store
- Point the camera at the QR code for a few seconds (no need to take a photo).
- A link should appear on the display, leading you to the location of the code

Bad Ems

SCAN HERE

HOW TO USE QR CODE

- Open your phone's camera app or download scanner app from play store or apple store
- Point the camera at the QR code for a few seconds (no need to take a photo).
- A link should appear on the display, leading you to the location of the code

Monschau

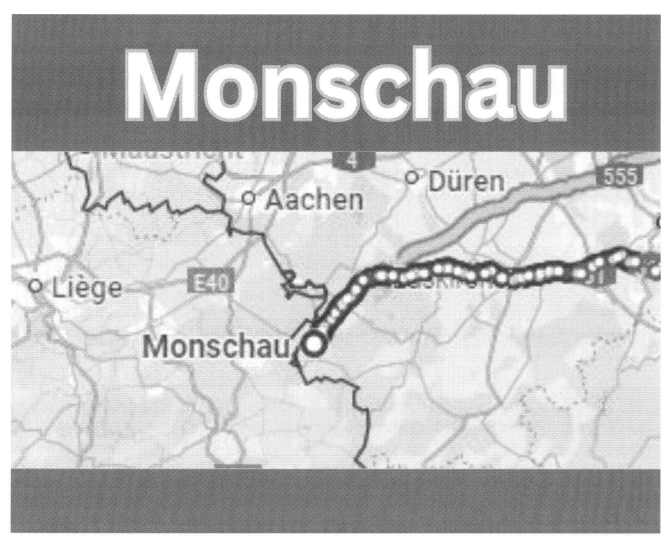

SCAN HERE

HOW TO USE QR CODE

- Open your phone's camera app or download scanner app from play store or apple store
- Point the camera at the QR code for a few seconds (no need to take a photo).
- A link should appear on the display, leading you to the location of the code

Meersburg

SCAN HERE

HOW TO USE QR CODE

- Open your phone's camera app or download scanner app from play store or apple store
- Point the camera at the QR code for a few seconds (no need to take a photo).
- A link should appear on the display, leading you to the location of the code

Görlitz

SCAN HERE

HOW TO USE QR CODE

- Open your phone's camera app or download scanner app from play store or apple store
- Point the camera at the QR code for a few seconds (no need to take a photo).
- A link should appear on the display, leading you to the location of the code

Chapter 8

Practical Travel Information & Safety Tips

Traveling in Germany is straightforward and convenient thanks to efficient transportation, modern infrastructure, and strong safety measures. Whether you're crossing borders, handling money, or planning a sustainable trip, here is a highlight of essential information to ensure a smooth experience.

We'll cover entry requirements currency tips, emergency contacts, eco-friendly travel, and recommended itineraries for various types of travelers.

Entry Requirements & Cross-Border Travel

Germany is part of the Schengen Area, allowing passport-free travel between 26 European countries.

1. Visa & Entry Requirements

EU/EEA citizens: No visa required; only an ID card or passport.

US, UK, Canada, Australia and New Zealand: Visa-free for stays up to 90 days within 180 days.

Other nationalities: May require a Schengen visa; check with the German consulate.

2. Border Crossings & Customs Regulations

Driving Across Borders: no border checks between Schengen countries, but carry your passport/ID and car documents.

Duty-Free Allowances: Limits on alcohol, tobacco, and luxury goods when bringing items into Germany.

Pet Travel: Pets need an EU pet passport, microchip, and rabies vaccination.

Tip: If traveling to Switzerland or the UK, customs checks apply as they are outside Schengen.

Currency, Payments, & ATMs

Germany uses the Euro (€), and while it's card-friendly, some places still prefer cash payments.

1. Using Cash vs. Cards

Cards Accepted: Most shops, hotels, and restaurants take Visa, Mastercard, and Maestro.

Cash is Still Common: Many small businesses, cafes, and local markets prefer cash.

Digital Payments: Google Pay & Apple Pay work in larger cities but not everywhere.

2. Where to Find ATMs & Exchange Money

ATMs (Geldautomaten): These are widely available in banks, train stations, and shopping centers.

Currency Exchange: This is available at airports, major train stations, and banks, but exchange rates are often better at ATMs.

Tip: Avoid ATMs in tourist areas, as they may have high fees use bank ATMs instead.

Emergency Numbers & Traveler Safety

Germany is a safe country, but it's still important to know emergency contacts and safety tips.

1. Important Emergency Numbers

☎ **112:** General emergency number for police, fire, and ambulance.

+49 89 22 22 22 (ADAC Roadside Assistance): For car breakdowns and towing services.

116 117: Non-emergency medical assistance.

2. Staying Safe While Traveling

Low Crime Rates: Violent crime is rare, but pick pocketing happens in crowded areas.

Secure Your Valuables: Keep your passport, money, and phone in a safe place.

Beware of Tourist Scams: Watch out for fake petitions, distraction theft, and ATM fraud.

Tip: If you lose your passport contact your embassy or consulate immediately.

Sustainable Travel Tips Eco Friendly Transportation Recycling, & Green Accommodations

Germany is a leader in sustainability, with efficient public transport, recycling programs, and eco-friendly hotels.

1. Green Transportation Options

Use Trains & Buses: The Deutsche Bahn (DB) train network is efficient & eco-friendly.

Rent a Bike: Cities like Berlin, Munich & Hamburg have excellent bike lanes & rentals.

Electric Car Rental: Companies like Sixt & Share Now offer electric vehicle rentals.

2. Recycling & Reducing Waste

Recycling Bins Everywhere: Follow Germany strict waste separation system.

Refillable Bottles: Tap water is safe to drink, reducing plastic waste.

Tip: Stay in eco-certified hotels, such as those with a Green Key or BioHotel certification.

Germany offers something for everyone, from fast-paced sightseeing tours to relaxing nature escapes.

1. One-Week Highlights: A Fast-Paced Road Trip

Day 1-2: Berlin: Brandenburg Gate, Museum Island, Berlin Wall.

Day 3: Dresden: Baroque architecture & Elbe River views.

Day 4-5: Munich & Neuschwanstein Castle: Bavarian charm & fairytale castles.

Day 6: The Rhine Valley: Vineyards & medieval castles.

Day 7: Cologne: Saint Mary Catholic Cathedral & vibrant old town.

2. Two-Week Culture & Nature Tour

Covers cities & scenic landscapes:

Berlin & Potsdam (history & culture)

Dresden & Saxon Switzerland (nature & hiking)

Nuremberg & Romantic Road (medieval towns)

Munich & the Alps (Bavarian culture)

Black Forest & Lake Constance (scenic nature)

Rhine Valley & Cologne (wine & castles)

3. Family-Friendly Road Trip

Perfect for kids & families

Legoland Deutschland (Günzburg)

Europa Park (Rust): Germany's biggest amusement park.

Berlin Zoo & Hamburg's Miniatur Wunderland.

Fairy Tale Route (Brothers Grimm Towns).

4. Luxury Travel Itinerary

Stay in castles & 5-star hotels; enjoy fine dining & exclusive experiences:

Brenners Park-Hotel (Baden-Baden) – Luxury spa retreat.

Schloss Elmau (Bavarian Alps) – High-end wellness resort.

Neuschwanstein Castle Private Tour – Exclusive VIP access.

Gourmet Dining – Michelin-star restaurants in Berlin, Munich & Hamburg.

5. Backpacker's Budget Guide

Affordable travel tips

Stay in hostels & budget hotels (A&O, Meininger, or Airbnb).

Use Flixbus & regional trains for cheap transport.

Eat at Bäckereien (bakeries) & Imbiss stalls for budget-friendly meals.

Take advantage of free walking tours & museum discount days.

Final Thoughts Travel Smart & Enjoy Germany

Germany is a safe, easy to navigate, and diverse travel destination. Whether you're backpacking on a budget exploring with family, or indulging in luxury, proper planning ensures a smooth and unforgettable trip.

Consider investing in practical tools such as local maps and travel apps that can enhance your exploration. Whether you're navigating public transport, discovering hidden gems off the beaten path, or simply trying to find the best local cuisine, being prepared will enrich your journey.

Traveling smart also means being aware of regional etiquette, respecting local traditions, and ensuring you leave a positive impact on the communities you visit. Sustainability should be at the forefront of your travel habits, supporting local businesses and being conscientious about your environmental footprint.

Germany is a land of unforgettable experiences waiting to be discovered. With careful planning and a willingness to explore, you can make memories that will last a lifetime. Happy travels!

The Fairytale Castle

Saint Mary Catholic Cathedral

Potsdam

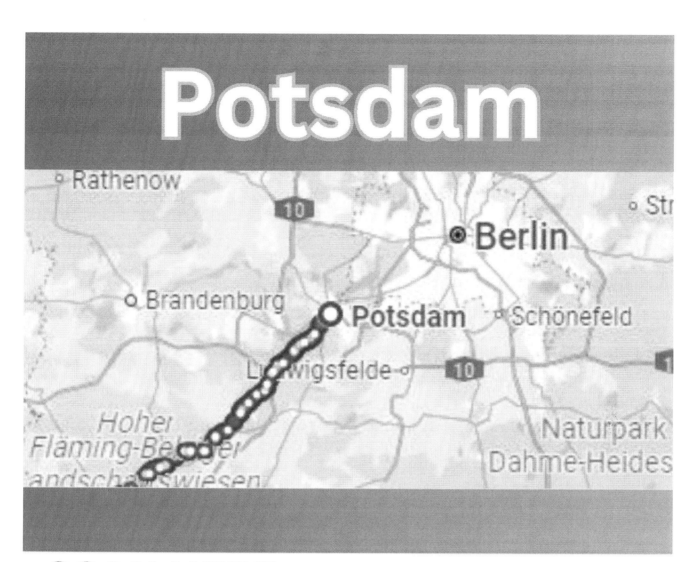

SCAN HERE

HOW TO USE QR CODE

- Open your phone's camera app or download scanner app from play store or apple store
- Point the camera at the QR code for a few seconds (no need to take a photo).
- A link should appear on the display, leading you to the location of the code

Europa-Park

Berlin Zoological Garden

Miniatur Wunderland

Brenners Park-Hotel & Spa

Schloss Elmau

Neuschwanstein Castle

Conclusion

Final Travel Tips

Germany is a country that rewards travelers with a perfect blend of history, culture, and breathtaking landscapes. Whether you're exploring bustling cities, scenic countryside, or charming medieval towns, a well-planned trip ensures a smooth and enjoyable experience.

As we wrap up this guide, let's recap the key takeaways for making the most of your journey, highlight essential resources, and encourage you to venture beyond the beaten path to uncover Germany's hidden gems.

Summary of Key Takeaways for Smooth Travel

1. Plan Your Route, But Stay Flexible

Germany offers well-maintained highways, scenic routes, and themed road trips that plan your primary destinations but leave room for spontaneous detours.

Consider a mix of big cities, small villages, and natural wonders to get the most out of your trip.

2. Understand the Road System

The Autobahn is famous for sections without speed limits, but always drive cautiously and observe posted signs.

Be aware of low-emission zones (Umweltzonen) in cities make sure your rental car complies.

Learn German road signs and regulations to ensure a smooth driving experience.

3. Choose the Best Transport Option for Each Destination

In cities like Berlin, Munich, and Hamburg, public transport is often easier than driving using trains, trams, and buses.

For longer distances, consider combining road trips with high-speed trains (ICE) to save time.

4. Book Accommodation in Advance (Especially in Peak Seasons)

Hotels, guesthouses, and vacation rentals offer various options for all budgets.

If you're planning a road trip with an RV or campervan, reserve campsites early, especially in summer.

Staying in small towns or countryside B&Bs can add a unique local experience.

5. Keep Essential Travel Documents Handy

Driver's license (an International Driving Permit may be required).

Car rental documents (insurance, emissions sticker if needed).

Passport/ID, and check if you need a Schengen visa.

Travel insurance for medical and emergency coverage.

6. Prepare for Different Payment Methods

Germany is increasingly card-friendly, but cash is still needed in rural areas, small shops, and local markets.

Have a credit/debit card with no foreign transaction fees and always carry some cash (€50-100) just in case.

7. Be Aware of Local Customs & Etiquette

Germans appreciate punctuality, so try to be on time for reservations, tours, and appointments.

Sundays are quiet days many shops are closed, but restaurants, cafes, and tourist sites remain open.

Tipping culture: Round up to the nearest euro or add 5-10% in restaurants.

8. Stay Safe & Informed

Germany is a safe country, but be aware of pickpockets in tourist areas.

Save emergency numbers (112 for police, fire, and ambulance).

Check travel alerts for road conditions, weather, and any local regulations before driving.

Maps, Navigation Apps, & Travel Websites

With modern technology and digital tools, navigating Germany has never been easier. Here are some must-have resources to keep your trip smooth and hassle-free.

1. Navigation & Map Apps

Google Maps: Best for navigation, walking routes, and real-time traffic updates.

Waze: Great for avoiding traffic jams and speed cameras.

Komoot: Ideal for hiking, cycling, and scenic route planning.

2. Public Transport & Rideshare Apps

DB Navigator (Deutsche Bahn) for train schedules & ticket bookings.

FlixBus: Budget-friendly long-distance bus travel.

Free Now & Bolt: Germany's alternative to Uber for taxis and ride-hailing.

3. Fuel & EV Charging Station Apps

Tank & Rast: Find gas stations and rest stops along the Autobahn.

Plugsurfing & EnBW mobility: Locate electric vehicle (EV) charging stations.

4. Accommodation Booking Platforms

Booking.com & Airbnb: Best for hotels, guesthouses, and vacation rentals.

Park4Night & ADAC Camping: Top apps for campsites and RV parking.

5. Weather & Safety Alerts

Wetter.com: Germany's most accurate weather forecast.

NINA App: Official app for emergency alerts, road closures, and weather warnings.

Tip: Download offline maps before your trip in case of poor mobile signal in rural areas.

Encouragement to Explore Beyond the Main Roads & Embrace the Unexpected

While Germany's major cities and famous landmarks are a must-see, some of the most rewarding experiences come from venturing beyond the tourist hotspots.

1. Take the Scenic Route

Instead of rushing between cities, explore the smaller roads and enjoy:

The Romantic Road, winding through medieval villages and fairytale castles.

The Moselle Valley where vineyard and river views make for an unforgettable drive.

The Black Forest High Road is a breathtaking journey through dense forests and rolling hills.

2. Stay in a Small Town or Village

Germany's smaller towns offer an authentic experience with historic charm and local traditions. Consider.

Rothenburg ob der Tauber: A perfectly preserved medieval town.

Monschau : A picturesque half-timbered village near the Eifel National Park.

Meersburg: A lakeside town with vineyards and stunning views of Lake Constance.

3. Try Regional Specialties & Local Markets

Each region has its own traditional food and drinks be sure to try.

Bavarian Weisswurst & pretzels in Munich.

Saxon Eierschecke cake in Dresden.

Schwarzwälder Kirschtorte (Black Forest Cake) in the Black Forest.

Fresh seafood on the North Sea coast in Hamburg.

4. Experience Local Festivals & Traditions

Germany is home to vibrant festivals throughout the year. If your trip aligns with these, don't miss.

Oktoberfest Munich: The world-famous beer festival (September- October).

Christmas Markets: From Nuremberg to Cologne, magical holiday markets in December.

Carnival (Cologne & Düsseldorf): A lively street festival full of costumes, parades, and music.

Tip: Be open to unexpected discoveries whether it's a small-town festival, a roadside café, or a breathtaking sunset over the Alps, some of the best moments happen when you least expect them.

Embrace the Journey

Germany is a country of contrasts, where history meets modernity and scenic landscapes meet dynamic cities. With a well-planned route, an open mind, and a sense of adventure, your trip will be unforgettable.

So, whether you're cruising on the Autobahn, hiking in the Alps, or exploring a historic town, remember:

Enjoy the ride

Take the scenic route

Savor the experiences

And most importantly, immerse yourself in the journey!

Happy travels!

Made in United States
Troutdale, OR
04/29/2025

30987945R00097